REASONS FOR TRUMP

BENJAMIN MARSHALL

© **2021** by Benjamin Marshall
Published by Passion Publications
a division of Tell the Truth International
7005 Woodbine Ave
Sacramento, Ca. 95822
tellthetruthsac@gmail.com
www.tttmi.org

Printed in the United States of America

All rights reserved. No part of this book may be reproduced in whole or part, in any form or by any means, electronic or mechanical, including photocopying, recording or by any information storage and retrieval system without express written permission from the author.

Cover image and design by:
charlyn_designs@fiverr.com

ISBN: 978-0-9729904-8-6

CONTENTS

Forward 5
Introduction 7
Complaints Against Trump 11
Proponents For Trump 23

His Person

Reason #1: He Is Not A Politician 25
Reason #2: He Does What He Says 27
Reason #3: He Is A Fighter 29
Reason #4: He Is Clear And Direct 30
Reason #5: He Is Secure 32
Reason #6: He Is A Business Man 34

His Values

Reason #7: He Is Pro-Life 36
Reason #8: He Is Pro-Traditional Family 38
Reason #9: He Is A Protecter 40
Reason #10: He Loves America 42
Reason #11: He Supports Individual Freedoms 44

His Policies

Reason #12: He Supports Religious Freedom 47
Reason #13: He Supports Military And Police 49
Reason #14: He Supports Educational Choice 51
Reason #15: His Foreign Policies Makes Sense 53
Reason #16: He Stimulates The Economy 54

His Assignment

Reason #17: God Chose Him 56
Reason #18: He Is Fulfilling Prophecy 57
Reason #19: He Supports Israel 58
Reason #20: He Does Not Follow The Global Agenda 60
Reason #21: He Is Fighting The Media For Truth 63

Response To Complaints 65
Role Of Media 75
Challenge To Christians 81
Election For Freedom 94
Final Summary 97
Bibliography 101
About The Author 104

FORWARD

Shouldn't we all be encouraged to live according to thoughts and beliefs that are not borrowed, but instead are our very own? Today, there are too many people whose personal beliefs, choices, and opinions are based on what somebody else has said or encouraged them to believe. The views given here are to assist individuals in their thinking process when considering a decision about Mr. Trump.

This book makes the effort to process the public opinions about Trump and his actions, weighing them with other considerations in understanding how people came to a solid conclusion without apology. Included are the complaints of many voters about Trump as a person and leader followed by twenty-one reasons why many others choose to support his efforts. This book can help those who are at a loss to comprehend how others could jump aboard the Trump train.

Finally, I share how my faith along with my life experiences has helped to shape my own political views as it relates to Mr. Trump. In addition, I give my thoughts about the faith community and some of their responses. It is my hope that each reader will get their own view, make their own argument, and take their own stand for the right reasons.

INTRODUCTION

In 2015, a man by the name of Donald J. Trump announced his run for office of the President of the United States. A man who had no previous political experience. He was a wealthy business entrepreneur, a real estate mogul, best known for the empire, grand buildings, and towers he built. Besides this, he was a force behind the Miss USA pageants. Lastly, he also was known as the boss in his own TV reality show called "The Apprentice."

He would be only one of two successful presidential candidates who never had any prior political experience or ever served in the U.S. military. In recent years, candidates such as Ross Perot and Herman Cain, also businessmen and political outsiders who ran in 1992 and 2012 respectively, saw some success in their bids for the presidency. However, hardly anybody believed Mr. Trump had any real shot at winning.

Amazingly, despite attacks against his personality, character, and previous failures brought out by the mainstream media and his political opponents, his message of "Making America Great Again" struck a chord with many. His challenge of "What do you have to lose with me?" was accepted by groups of voters.

What in the world did people see in him? Why would so many go against conventional knowledge and take such a risk with someone so inexperienced among other things? He surprisingly won the nomination of his party easily and was given no chance of winning the presidency against a seasoned politician named Clinton.

After having gone through many accusations - some true, perhaps many overblown, and some not so true by the opposing party and media forces - his message prevailed again. He was voted in as our 45th president. Since that time, he has endured massive criticism, Russia collusion accusations, impeachment attempts, Covid-19, and a controversial re-election. Throughout it all, the Trump train seems to surprisingly keep gaining steam and more passengers are jumping on.

The fact is, he is an anomaly in politics. There has never been anything like Trump before and I doubt we will ever see anything like him again. It is hard to find an American voter who is in the middle about him. People either love him or hate him. He produces strong feelings and reactions from even the most uninformed citizens.

Like myself, many have been voting since they were old enough to vote. Citizens normally vote for the candidate who they believe best represents their beliefs and convictions. People want someone who will support and fight for the things they cherish the most. With political figures, it is hard to find someone who will support all or most of the things you deem important. For example: a pro-life candidate who promises to support legislation to protect unborn children in the womb might also sign legislation that tries to remove guns from citizens. Perhaps there is a candidate who fights for traditional family values and defends a person's moral conscious but supports imprisoning the most vulnerable for petty things with few reform opportunities. Another candidate may support affordable medical for all but places a low priority on our military defense. They may favor fighting a war to defend democracy with our troops around the world while not taking care of our veterans at home. Sometimes it can be challenging to choose the right candidate. So, all we can do is our best.

The things we personally value most, will help to decide who our candidate choice will be. We must prioritize the issues that are most important and that we refuse to compromise on. These may include any of the following: economic stimulus, foreign policy, health care, military issues, constitutional issues, judicial selections, gun policy, racial equality, immigration, abortion, environment and climate change, traditional family values, religious liberty, protection of moral consciousness, law enforcement, more individual freedom, and less government. All these issues are important because we are affected by them and the decisions made pertaining to them. Therefore, we must resolve in our minds and hearts what we value most and vote accordingly.

We are also impacted by how a candidate makes us feel, and his or her likability. Many decide based on whether they believe the candidate has proven character or whether the candidate looks and acts presidential (outward appearance and behavior). It can be tough when one does not always have personal knowledge of the candidate, rather must rely on information about them from media and others. We then must look at their track record to determine what they have said and done to make a judgement as to whether they earn our respect and vote. Recently, our nation has been greatly divided on many issues, but probably none greater than the man himself, Donald J. Trump.

COMPLAINTS AGAINST TRUMP

As an author, I thought it would be important to let my readers know regardless of what side they have taken, whether they support Mr. Trump or not, both sides should be heard. Many for him, are not unaware or have closed their eyes to the obvious offenses and reasonable doubts many citizens have about his personhood.

After we have reviewed both sides, I will share my own responses to these complaints, compare the pro's and con's, and my conclusion.

Many assume that a vote for Mr. Trump is agreement to everything that he has done, is doing, and will ever do. They may also think it is enabling him to continue in questionable activity without restraint or one does not care about the topic matter at all. On the contrary, many people have taken all into account and have battled personally to process correctly the hardest of truths in coming to their decision. Cries of hurt feelings, anger, and fear from his opponents have been heard by many Trump supporters. Here are several highly publicized complaints for review.

HE IS DIVISIVE

Many believe that one of the main jobs of the president is to make sure we have as much national unity as possible. To some, the president appears to be taking sides. "I want a president who doesn't help divide us but bring us together," reported one voter. Opponents say Mr. Trump's comments divide our nation into groups that fight and work against each other. They claim when he has opportunities to bring peace, his words fuel the fire of division, and he is unable to bring opposite sides together.

They point out the differences our nation has between groups like rural and city folks, men and women, young and old, conservatives and liberals, and white evangelicals and black mainline denominations. They accuse the president of trying to turn Americans against one another. In their estimation, he is putting further distance between the rich and poor; and is a dangerous threat to the country.

A White America

In addition to certain groups in our population, senators and other respected government officials have made statements implying Mr. Trump's stances support the spread of racism and white nationalism. He has been accused of trying to make America white again and weaken diversity. Instead of strengthening our differences, they believe he uses our differences for his own advancement.

Is he the president for a white America? Is that what he means by making America great again? Rather than viewing his slogan as a great thing, they view it as dangerous ideology. It has been labeled as a hate filled agenda that goes against democracy, justice, and dignity.

Mr. Trump has also been accused of catering to certain sectors such as older white males, wealthy business owners, and white evangelicals. It is believed he is advancing their agenda while ignoring other groups. They find and point to things they feel support their beliefs. For example, his cabinet and administration positions: majority white males, less diversity than previous administrations, with only one African American and no Hispanics represented as cabinet heads. Some say he represents that "good old boy" network while using rhetoric to awaken a spirit of a white superior ruling class.

Diversity

Other opponents accuse him of being on a mission to purge this nation from as many immigrants and minorities as possible. They say the diversity, freedom, and opportunities that make us a great country is in danger. He is blamed as the reason for societal conflicts and dividing America into a civil war atmosphere between blacks and whites, minorities and majority, and law enforcement and human right groups.

They point to the rise of protesting anti-groups, Trump's tweets, responses, and other mainstream media news stories to support their claims. Due to all of this, he has been painted by many as the enemy of diversity and freedom for the nation.

HE IS A RACIST

"Proud boys stand back and stand by." This was the response given by Mr. Trump at a press conference regarding a group, who many believe stand for white supremacy. They were on one side of a rioting incident in Charlottesville, Virginia, where a black woman was killed.

One lady told me this was the nail in the coffin for her. She said this statement was more than enough proof of his racism and gave her no reason at all to believe anything else. "Too many times," she blurted, "He had an opportunity to stand against white supremacy, K.K.K., and other bigots with his words and actions, but he refused." His comment further adding, "There were good people on both sides," was considered even worse. These things are interpreted as proof of racism. "He is blatantly racist," another said. It is fair to assess this as representative of how other fellow Americans feel.

Critics feel his comments and actions do not reflect American values. They are convinced his words and policies attack religious and ethnic minorities such as Muslims, Black Americans, and native Africans. Couple this with complaints by others who swear he does not like Hispanics; no wonder such a huge case has been built against him in this area.

People are quick to point attention for proof to Trump's ban on Muslim nations, the Deferred Action for Childhood Arrivals (DACA) program where he tried to send refugees (in the Temporary Protected Status program) back home. He has been quoted as referring to African nations as shit-hole countries. They say there have been incidences that suggest it is more than accidental with him, but a patterned lifestyle from discrimination lawsuits against him as early as the 70's to the challenging of Obama on his citizenship after he produced what appeared to be a legitimate certificate proving his U.S. birth.

His critics say he has made a point of focusing on the identity of Mexicans and their ancestry during disagreements which have no bearing on the business at hand. For example: a controversy with a lawyer combating a court case of his in the past. He has demonized Mexican immigrants by stating many who cross our borders are rapists and drug dealers. His rivals also point to his zero-tolerance approach on border issues without empathy which allowed the separation of Hispanic children from their families in overcrowded detention facilities.

From Trump's reference to the coronavirus as the "Chinese" virus or "kung flu" to his description of Elizabeth Warren as "Pocahontas" - referring to her Native American claim, critics agree these racial slurs should be condemned. Lastly, to seal the deal for their overwhelming proof of him being racist, his opponents point to his support of restrictions on racial sensitivity training.

HE ABUSES WOMEN

His adversaries say he has referred to women in a demeaning manner and views them as sex objects. The proof given is that Donald Trump is on record many times for having insulting feuds with women, inappropriate responses at his pageants, and using language with friends that suggest lewd comments and insults are a part of who he is.

Donald Trump publicly apologized for a taped conversation where he was caught making obscene remarks. He stated it was locker room talk and it was wrong. The publicity surrounding this exposure created outrage for many people, particularly groups of women activists for whom this cemented in their minds the kind of man they already believed him to be.

Another incident that was publicized against him was regarding a tweet made about four minority Congresswoman when he suggested, after their criticisms, they leave the U.S. and return to their respective countries of heritage where the governments are a complete unacceptable catastrophe.

Critics who oppose Mr. Trump want to ensure the public believes that what has been said or done by him in the past is still true for today. There are reference pages of numerous quotes that include sexist remarks along with recordings by Trump available on public news pages.

HE IS A LIAR

"The president is a liar," exclaimed one lady I spoke with. "He won't admit to obvious mistakes. Her comrades agreed, "He continually makes claims that are not true. He lied about Mexico paying for the wall. He lied by downplaying the Coronavirus and putting our nation at more of a health risk." Her cohorts added to the list, "What about the economy, Russia, and China?" From their list, the accusations go on and on.

Antagonists agree many of his statements reflect beliefs that are false, misleading, and taken out of context. He is blamed for not being informed and repeatedly under playing, overstating, and exaggerating things when communicating. His critics say they can disprove most of what he says.

He has made mistakes about places and locations, from building the wall and protecting borders in Colorado (not a border state) to referring to Iran as Iraq during an airstrike. One person I know shared, "I don't want a president that doesn't know his geography."

HE DOESN'T DISPLAY LEADERSHIP CHARACTER

It was during a debate with Secretary of State and Democratic nominee Hilary Clinton that she said, "I usually never question someone's character for this job, but Donald Trump is not fit to be president." By her standards of the character needed to hold the highest office in the land, he failed miserably in her opinion and in the estimation of a high percentage of her followers.

The ability to lead and the character to lead is not the same. These people do not question that he is a leader, but they question his character to be a successful leader of our nation.

What qualities do people look for in a president? There are many we can name, but his rivals seem to allude to the integrity issue, which speaks more to moral uprightness. Is he going to do the right things, say the right things, and stand for the right things? In their unanimous opinion, No! Next, they believe he is lacking the necessary humility, collaboration, and empathy to do the job that is required as a leader of a country like America. When there is such a diverse population of people representing so many different cultures, many want to have a leader who can consider all groups and view life from their perspectives and be willing to share in their feelings and struggles. Many, on the opposing side, do not believe this is the case.

Many of his counterparts find his references to other people, outside of their names, as juvenile and unprofessional. Instead of being amused, they see it as sarcastic and mocking rhetoric. They feel it is demeaning and that it tells you a lot about the true character of a man. Trump is known for nicknaming all his rivals and critics. For example: Pocahontas Warren, sleepy Joe Biden, low energy Jeb, wild Bill, and crooked Hilary. Other adjectives he has used to describe his nemesis are lightweight, phony, puppet, corrupt, cheating, weird, wacko, little, crazy, and goofy.

HE HAS A BAD TEMPERAMENT

He is considered brash, arrogant, mouthy, pushy, and rude by opponents. "It is a good thing that someone with the temperament of Donald Trump is not over our law enforcement," presidential candidate Hilary Clinton said during a 2016 presidential debate. Mr. Trump responded, "Because you'd be in jail." These and many other moments are used to define the man known as Donald Trump for many people

Antagonists view him as a man with a seriously frowned, unpleasant disposition who is fiery, wild, off- the-cuff, and "in your face" kind of guy. In a recent debate with 2020 Democratic nominee Joe Biden, it was hard for Biden to finish a sentence or get a word in without being interrupted and interrogated by Trump. Like a pit bull with a poodle, Biden seemed to have no chance against what many rivals call a bully. Totally frustrated, Biden finally told the president, "Will you shut up man?"

His outspoken judgements and demeanor have caused his opponents to see him as totally out of control, hard to deal with, and so strongly opinionated that he is unable to accomplish much of anything with his peers. They state the belittling of others, regular attacks, continually defending himself, and stigmatization of other people and groups will never endear him to a mass base. They believe this results in keeping an already divided nation from ever coming together.

Opposers say, they cannot help but to continually worry and question: How many of his decisions will be irrational? How will they negatively impact us? Will his mouth get our nation in trouble with foreign world powers?

HE IS A DICTATOR

Mr. Trump's enemies describe him as demanding, dictatorial, and authoritarian. They believe he uses his position to implement what he wants and those things that further his own agenda at the expense of everyone else. He is accused of abusing his power. This type of accusation is what led to his impeachment trial. He has also been called crybaby, stubborn, and insistent. It is said, he pushes his agenda without being willing to negotiate reasonably.

People point to the high turnover in government under his watch and feedback from disgruntled former employees who previously worked for him as proof of a dictatorial leader. Before getting involved in a political career, Trump was widely known for his reality show, *The Apprentice;* and the phrase "You're fired." Since taking office as President, there has been a considerable amount of changing of the guard from chiefs of staffs, ambassadors, directors, security advisors and aides, secretary's, communication's staff, attorney generals, campaign personnel, strategist, health directors, FBI staff, and press staff.

Some are said to be volunteer resignations, but many appear to be terminations or forced resignations. Opponents point to this as support of a toxic, chaotic leader who follows to the beat of his own drum at the expense of the good for the whole. A leader that says it will be done my way or you hit the highway.

PROPONENTS FOR TRUMP

21 REASONS WHY

Despite numerous complaints on one side of the coin, Trump's supporters on the other side view him very differently. There is a mass following who are pro-Trump for many different reasons. Although many wish he wasn't so abrasive, they are not willing to stop standing behind him because of this or for any of the other reasons previously listed. A person might be thinking, what reasons could they possibly have that could outweigh the previous complaints? Here are twenty-one reasons why Donald Trump is supported by over 70 million voters. It will be divided up into four segments: his person, his values, his policies, and his assignment.

HIS PERSON

REASON #1

HE IS NOT A POLITICIAN

What's wrong with a politician? Nothing. Why does it matter? It matters because it does definitely change some things. This makes him extremely unique as a president. As someone who has never served in the military or held any public office, he truly is an outsider to a very selected group in government affairs. This reason could be seen as a major disadvantage, but many see it as a major advantage.

Advantages include: He is not prone to play political games. He doesn't play by the rules of the establishment, nor is he apart of it. He hasn't been trained how to lie in politics or be politically correct. He is not a part of the establishment. He can approach issues as one who is representing the interests of an average citizen like himself. He has had success outside of politics. He knows how to succeed without the assistance of special interest or lobby groups. He is not bought. He doesn't need to accept other people's money or assistance to be elected in exchange for favors once in office. He has not sacrificed his views on the altar of the party for support, but uses the party platform to share his own views.

Disadvantages include: He was not familiar with the way things worked in government. He had no experience. He wasn't as informed about existing policies. He does not have political etiquette.

The way these shortcomings are being responded to are: He places competent people who are capable of leading in capacities where he is not as strong. In unfamiliar areas, he learns from informants, advisers, and teachers.

In both instances, this is not a con but a pro for his supporters. He represents a voice in government for the people. He is an American citizen who is as far away from political assimilation as one of us can get, yet is sitting in the highest office of the land.

REASON #2

HE DOES WHAT HE SAYS

Experts will acknowledge, when you look at the decades of time it usually takes for someone who has been sitting in high government offices to accomplish things, Trump's effort and pace have been unbelievable. Supporters say he has not wasted time, immediately coming into office, and actively working for the American people; attempting to get as much done as possible. This has been incredible, they say, when you consider that he is working with so many people in Congress who loathe him.

His advocates continue, many can not say they have seen him say one thing and do another in regards to what he wants to do. His pursuits and actions have been pretty consistent with what comes out of his mouth. The question of whether he will follow through on his promises have been answered. Under his administration there were fast legislation changes, along with a better economy.

It is refreshing for his supporters to know there is going to be something done. If you have ten things on your to do list and you get five done, you would probably be a very happy person. Many are satisfied with the results of his first term as president. Trump has produced results, even if everything he set out to do hasn't been completed.

The fact is: When you do what you say you are going to do, people believe in you. When they see you making an attempt to do it, even if you fail, it speaks volumes to them. If you ask them to give you time, people are willing to give you time. The more you get done, the more time they are willing to give you to get other things done. The bottom line is people don't want to hear excuses, they want to see actions that correlate with your words. Trumps supporters like what he promised during his campaign and what he has done in office.

REASON #3

HE IS A FIGHTER

Many people don't want somebody who does everything right, they want someone who won't give up until certain things are done. Trump is seen as one who is focused. His supporters feel like he knows what he wants and is going to find a way to make it happen. He is willing to take on the world. He is willing to be unpopular, criticized, take risks, and fail. He is not intimidated. He is not going to give up easily. He will not quit. He is persistent, unrelenting, and will do whatever he feels he needs to. He is going to take hit after hit and confidently move forward like an unstoppable force.

Trump makes his supporters think he can win in everything. He seems to enjoy a good fight. Many Americans want someone they believe will stand up and fight for their beliefs, rights, and wellbeing as citizens. Trump will let you know you are in a fight and people like that. "If I was going to have a person fight for me, I would want someone with his tenacity," someone voiced. He won't let distractions block him from completing the goals he made. This is who many people want leading them.

Lastly, almost everybody likes an underdog. People can relate to being counted out and having to overcome insurmountable odds. People are saying, "Let's see how he will prove everybody wrong this time." He is the Rocky of politics. It always appears he is going to lose, but he finds a way to win with a last minute knock out.

REASON #4

HE IS CLEAR AND DIRECT

Trump advocates love that he is never at a loss for words and can be easily understood. They don't have to guess what he is thinking because he will tell you if you ask him. They say, people may not like what he says, but they will be sure of what he thinks. He is direct, simple, and clear. There isn't any need for an interpreter. He is someone that you can follow along with; someone a child can understand.

His supporters add that he doesn't play games with his words. He doesn't tell people what he thinks they want to hear. He is sharing how he really feels and how he wants others to hear it. He is not attempting to appeal to one's emotions. Trump's speeches are characterized as authentic, heartfelt, and direct to his listeners.

Trumps outspoken and opinionated approach may appear inappropriate to some, but many supporters appreciate his bold approach. His supporters are not quick to blame him for things he says. They rather focus on "What was the context surrounding those words." When opponents ask, "Did you hear what he said?" Supporters respond, "Yes, but I also see what he is doing. I don't react to what you think he is saying, I respond to what he ultimately does."

Whether you see his approach as a strength or weakness, his supporters will rather allow him to be who he is than to do without him. They insist the value of good outweighs the bad. Like medicine, it may not taste good going down, but it will accomplish the purpose. They see him like a prescription Americans need, the side effects are just small irritations to the greater goal.

REASON #5

HE IS SECURE

Eventhough it appears he doesn't care if you like him, his supporters are not foolish to believe that nothing gets to him. It is human to have an aversion to criticism. Everybody's sensitivity point is at a different level. Mr. Trump is comfortable enough with himself to move forward in spite of the constant criticisms directed at him. It takes some people many, many years to find out who they are, accept themselves, and be without apologizing for it. Many people struggle with insecurity and answering the questions: Who am I? Do I like me? Do I believe in me? Nobody can be their best if they are dependent on others liking them. People are attracted to people who know who they are, where they are going, and what they want to do. Without having this self confidence, it would be difficult to succeed, influence others, and gain respect.

Advocates believe that he is a secure president. He is not trying to win a popularity contest. He is secure enough to handle criticism and fight back. His goal is not for people to like him, but he has decided if he stands for what he believes is right and for the American people, than he will appeal to the people and his message will resonate with them. He is focused on accomplishing the mission he is on. This is a breath of fresh air for those who are tired of political antics.

His followers love his confidence. They love the fact he doesn't need constant validation or approval and doesn't accommodate everybody nor try to please them. He is true to who he is. He can handle a lost, but he doesn't like to lose. They dont want to follow a leader who doesn't care if he loses. Trump's hopes, dreams, and optimism for a better America and willingness to take on all challenges has endeared him to a mass following.

REASON #6

HE IS A BUSINESS MAN

Many of his backers have stated, "We need someone who knows how to take care of business." We need a president who understands money, how to put people in position to get things done, and how to replace ineffective people without letting their feelings or other influences get in the way. We need someone who will put the business affairs of the nation before friendships, who can't be bought, and who understands the bottom line is, *What is in the best interest of Americans?*

His supporters say Trump has had undeniable success as a business man. His success carried into the presidency as made evident by the booming economy under his leadership. He has reworked deals with foreign nations that now favor America. He has the respect, even if disliked, of world leaders such as Putin and Jung. He's tough when dealing with China and joint nation councils when it comes to economics. He doesn't back down or accept being taken advantage of. This is the kind of commander-in-chief so many people were excited about and envisioned before casting their vote for him.

HIS VALUES

REASON #7

HE IS PRO-LIFE

Many believe life is is a God-given right; only He can give it and take it away. Pro-life advocates are convinced anything done to prevent life from continuing inside a woman's womb as well as after birth is nothing short of murder. Many believe we must not abort any human life. Many people choose those who value life in the womb to represent them.

This critical issue of the sanctity of life is a basic one and Mr. Trump has demonstrated by his actions that he not only believes in the sanctity of life, but is willing to protect and defend this important value that many share. He is anti-abortion. This issue alone was a major deciding factor in a large percentage of people backing him. There are many people who are more passionate about their stance on this topic than him.

Taking into consideration cases of rape, incest, or endangering a mother's life, Mr. Trump has expressed support for banning abortion. He has been quoted as saying, he would like to see Roe vs Wade overturned, it should be more difficult to get an abortion, and there should be no federal protections for the procedure. He curtailed federal funding as promised so no federal family planning dollars are alloted to organizations that provide abortions or refer patients to abortion clinics. Planned parenthood lost millions in federal funds under his watch. He placed pro-life judges in the courts. He supported the stoppage of medical research using tissues of aborted babies. He urged the ban of late term abortion. He banned funding to organizations providing abortion overseas and he was the very first president to speak at the March of Life rally.

REASON #8

HE IS PRO-TRADITIONAL FAMILY

Family is the basic foundational structure for any society. As the family's goes, so goes the nation. Many fans have noticed that Trump has on occasion defended the country from promoting laws affecting all families if it only favors a small minority. For example: He rescinded the guidelines and rights for transgender students to use bathrooms of the gender they identified with in the schools. He supported policies in the military that implemented restrictions to protect traditional gender roles. He refused to make transgender identity a focal point without violating a person's choice

Like many of his supporters, he supports traditional marriage. Although he is not a supporter of alternative marriage ideas, he has not discriminated by putting policies in place to conform people in believing, behaving, or accepting his ideas. He believes each state should decide and govern what happens regarding the social laws in their respective areas.

Healthcare is very important to many citizens. Trump made a commitment to replace Obamacare. During his first years in office, he proposed several replacements; none were approved by Congress. The president has recognized the importance of affordable alternative health care that includes existing conditions while lowering premiums and pharmaceutical costs. He was able to remove the tax law that penalized citizens who did not go along with a required government health care plan.

The president implemented measures to further combat human trafficking and online child exploitation. He created a fulltime position dedicated to fighting and preventing this evil. His administration approved a $35 million grant allocation from its Justice Department to provide housing for trafficking survivors.

President Trump signed into law "The First Step Act." This legislation introduced much needed reform to a broken criminal justice system. Many men and women have been on the receiving end of unfair prison sentences for years. This legislation allows nonviolent offenders a second chance to be productive citizens in our society. Prisoners can have sentences reduced and be released earlier based on good behavior. The bill is an effort to fix punitive prison sentences given in the federal courts. Since a high proportion were black men, their families have been severely impacted. Supporters believe this is a win for our country, especially our children who need their fathers at home.

REASON #9

HE IS A PROTECTER

President Trump's supporters believe he not only looks out for basic freedoms, takes care of our troops, and offers assistance to governors and mayors to quell violent protest in various cities, but insists on protecting the borders from outsiders. From the outset of his campaign to become president, Mr. Trump shared his concern about open borders and our inability to keep out undocumented immigrants, especially from Mexico. He vowed a zero tolerance policy and the building of a wall to secure our borders.

He was accused of being anti-Hispanic, but his supporters believe he only wants everyone to enter legally. They believe President Trump's priority has been the safety of all Americans first. He understands the border has been a major issue. He wants people to feel safe and secure in their own country. Many supporters like the fact that he wants to secure our country from illegal outsiders entering the country with no way of being tracked. They believe in order take part in the American dream, one should enter through legal means alone.

The Muslim ban also makes it more difficult for people to come from many countries illegally. Restrictions have been put in place to make it more difficult period. His advocates say his attempt to eliminate programs that favor immigrants and refugees are only to keep non-citizens from enjoying this nation's privileges if they are not willing to take the required legal steps.

The truth is, living in a country with open borders without protection, is scary for many people. Many Americans don't want the country carrying the responsibility of illegal immigrants or rewarding those who refuse to follow the legal process to enter the country. Although many are sympathetic to reasons why people make every effort to come to America, supporters feel we must enforce laws and use more stringent measures with foreigners entering this country.

REASON #10

HE LOVES AMERICA

In Donald J. Trump, many saw a man who did not care about a status quo, power, or wealth, but an American who loved America and was sick and tired of seeing the country destroyed by career politicians and empty promises. Supporters believe Mr. Trump ran because he believed he could help America. His actions demonstrated he cared about what happens to this nation and the people in it.

He appeared to his supporters to be a man who saw America losing to foreign countries, jobs leaving the country, and businesses hurting due to high taxes. He saw hardworking Americans frustrated and the economy at a standstill. He promised to rework deals and pass legislations that would favor Americans. He saw the inability to enforce immigration rules and protect our borders and the decaying of what was once a strong military, while our troops were sent to fight endless wars in other places.

Trump speaks against the socialistic move in our government that supports the erosion of the most basic individual rights and freedoms of its citizens. He is a non-politician fighting for the people and not the government. He speaks of America in a positive reaffirming way and celebrates all that is good about the country. He is extremely defensive of all who speak negatively or disrespects the USA. He appeals to patriots especially military veterans. He has made the rebirth of America and its sovereignty his focus while shifting attention away from globalism. He has vowed to appoint judges who follow the constitution of America given by its founders.

Trump courageously exposes corruption in our government and media. He is committed to freedom and justice in our country. Many Americans chose to follow a man that loves the nation and its people above the establishment, regardless of his human flaws.

REASON #11

HE SUPPORTS INDIVIDUAL FREEDOMS

President Trump supports freedom of moral conscious, freedom of speech, and the right to bear arms. He supports the American Constitution and Bill of Rights.

His administration supported a U.S. Supreme Court case, where an individual's right to free speech and religious exercise was challenged. The case involved a baker refusing to bake a cake for a gay couple's wedding. This support is also seen in legislation that doesn't mandate health workers to participate against their will in abortions. At some point, mandated covid vaccinations may become an issue. Advocates for Trump believe, with him as the leader, they will have the freedom to make their own decisions without pressure.

It appears Trump has ensured our federal laws do not allow gains in legislation that favor a particular minority group. One executive order requires free speech to always be allowed at universities in order to receive federal and research funding.

He supports a free market economy that helps owners, starts more ventures, and causes growth. He believes in the concept of ownership as a good thing and excessive regulations in businesses as a hinderance. He signed legislation that removed unnecessary regulations for businesses.

As seen by signed policies, Trump is an advocate for less government involvement in personal citizen matters. He supports freedom for individuals to live a life without numerous restraints. He trusts the American people to make decisions concerning their own lives without excessive dictates. He stays away from socialist systems. He supports reducing taxes for Americans, believing less taxes leave people and business with more money to invest and build the lives they desire. It also allows the economy to grow. On the other hand, paying more tax money to government gives them more control. He believes that Americans should keep more of their income. He is against the misuse of taxpayers money at the federal level and advocates for more accountability. This appeals to many Americans.

HIS POLICIES

REASON #12

HE SUPPORTS RELIGIOUS FREEDOM

Over the last decade prior to his presidency, hostility towards those of Christian faith has slowly began to rise; and there was less tolerance for those who take a conservative stand on moral issues. There has been a push to change people or re-educate people who won't adapt to the moral compass of the progressive agenda in our society. This has been evident in the difficulty to practice one's own faith within personal guidelines at work, at school, and other public places. There has been a pressing to override moral consciousness connected to religious beliefs in regards to medicine, education, and lifestyles. People of faith want to be able to practice freely their faith without intimidation or being forced to comply to things that go against it.

Respect and support are shown to other organizations, but against many faith based groups. This is witnessed in the right to assemble in certain places, share ideas, give speeches at graduations, and pray in public gatherings. People of faith want to have a voice and not be silenced or intimidated into quietness. Trump has fought for their rights to express themselves and do their mission.

President Trump supports the right for students to pray and have Bible study groups in school without retaliation. He believes in the fundamental right for every America to follow their religious convictions. His religious liberty act was signed so all religions would be treated equal by the government. This nation was birthed with Judeo-Christian principles and values, as seen and heard throughout its documents, songs, and on its currency. Phrases like, "One nation under God." "In God we trust." and "Unalienable rights given by the Creator." His followers take delight in this support.

REASON #13

HE SUPPORTS MILITARY AND POLICE

Trump has invested in making sure we have a strong military and as a country we take care of our veterans. He has demonstrated his seriousness to defend the nation from all enemies here and abroad.

According to his advocates, the national security is no longer threatened by a less strengthened military. He has made our military a priority investing millions in upgrades. As a strong advocate for the military and American's protection, he has successively completed missions against ISIS, which we hardly hear about anymore. He has worked to remove military from fighting endless wars abroad. There has been over 100,000 soldiers who have returned home under his leadership.

His Veteran's Mission Act, which permanently enables needed care anywhere for veterans who have served in the military, was a transformative act. He also forgave student debt for permanently disabled U.S. veterans. He overhauled the VA with legislation to make sure veteran families receive the assistance they need.

Trump is a believer in law and order. He supports supports Law enforcement and safety. As a result he earned the support of a police union representing over 300,000 members. Incidences of police brutality and racial injustice shouldn't be the basis for defunding police as a whole as some have suggested. His supporters agree with him that these are exceptions. Many Americans would rather have a strong presence of police protecting our communities. Also, respect for those in authority need to be modeled for future generations.

The president has said he wants to prosecute those who attack law officers. Many of his supporters think not only should there be public support for our officers, but also for appointed court and elected officials who will support measures that allow officers to do their jobs better.

REASON #14

HE SUPPORTS EDUCATIONAL CHOICE

Trump's free choice for education has been seen in different ways. Trump values vocational training. He eliminated cuts for vocational programs and increased career and technical funding. He increased funds to support school choice and expand charter schools. He continually emphasizes authority at the state level. His administration gave 85 million to the DC opportunity scholarship program to allow students to attend private schools.

One of the largest, school choice adversary, is the Public School Teacher Unions and their lobby groups. Some concerned parents believe the teacher's union only support leaders who will protect what's most important to them: money, tenure, and retirement; the needs of children are secondary. Many concerned parents believe the public education system and its agenda has been the greatest influence of liberalism for this current generation. They would like to have more input in their children's learning.

President Trump believes education should follow this protocol: 1) Put student's needs first with more control and choices for students and families. 2) Empower states to address their own needs. The states should spend money their way without much federal control. 3) There should be limited federal control. The federal education budget request should be limited. We should put more focus on people and less on paperwork. He believes this will give us better results.

He reduced federal authority over state K-12 education and slashed funding for underperforming after-school and teacher development programs. He signed measures to assist with college loan forgiveness. He provided for the distribution of Pell grants year-round and reduced the federal works study.

He gained additional minority support after championing for black colleges. His "Future Act" allotted 255 million for minority colleges. Historically Black College Universities (HBCU) received 85 million annually. With an impending end to certain funding, HBCU's received permanent funding through the Future Act. President Trump signed bills to increase overall funding and certain yearly funding without the worry of begging that these colleges had to do previously. The previous administration's budget cuts and limited parent plus loans hurt HBCU's enrollment.

Trump's administration cancelled repayment of 300 million in federal relief loans for four HBCU's who needed help after Hurricane Katrina in 2005. They fought for eight years to have this massive debt absolved and nothing had happened. He ended discriminatory restrictions to prevent faith based HBCU's from getting federal support and his administration provided millions in emergency relief for HBCU's during Covid-19.

Trump spoke at the White House HBCU week conference, inviting all presidents, chancellors, and leaders. He made HBCU's a priority and helped them in the press. The cause and effect of his advocacy reaches even farther. HBCU's can now prevent closures and provide employment opportunities. They can also have more renewals, sponsors, and grant support because of federal and state funding. His supporters would love to know why a so-called racist would do this.

REASON #15

HIS FOREIGN POLICIES MAKES SENSE

Trump supporters believe we are much stronger and our national security is better under his leadership. People may suggest that America take a greater role in many humanitarian issues while keeping an eye on what other nations and world leaders are doing, but Trump has decided to focus on America. Many Americans want to know, How can we help others around the world when we haven't fixed our own issues from within?

Looking at the highlights of his diplomatic dealings: He has reduced our reliance on China. He has dealt tough with them and North Korea. He confronted Iran and in 2018 pulled the United States out of the Iran nuclear agreement, which he promised to do during his campaign. He has not backed down from Russia and Mr. Putin. We have had no major terrorism threats from the Middle East since his order to kill Qassim Suleimani and other militia networks. He also committed to go after leaders or financers of terrorist groups. Our relations with Israel are better than ever.

REASON #16

HE STIMULATES THE ECONOMY

Trump's backers will tell you the nation has enjoyed a great economy under his leadership. There were four million jobs created since he has been in office. This has resulted in more employment with almost a half million manufacturing jobs produced. With this growth, we saw lower unemployment claims, especially among minorities, while the wages for earners increased.

The nation experienced tax relief, cuts and reforms, small businesses had their tax rate lowered, health plans were preserved by employers, and increases in prices for prescription drugs stopped. There were lower taxes for the wealthy, support and increase in the country's natural energy sources, and support for farmers. There was more production of energy sources like ethanol which means less dependence on foreign sources. We were the largest supplier of gas, oil and energy to the world. Our growth of wind and solar power accelerated while President Trump placed tariffs on imported solar cells. Many voters said this topic was the most important in deciding who they would vote for.

HIS ASSIGNMENT

REASON #17

GOD CHOSE HIM

Despite his human flaws, many saw something in Donald Trump that others could not see. Testimony after testimony, I heard others say, "God told me" or "Showed me" he is supposed to be president of the United States. People who share their own personal experience about God speaking to them, especially about this subject, can expect a collection of eyebrows raised, rolling eyes, and a quip "I'm sure He did." For the average person this sounds absurd. They would view you as a crazy super religious fanatic. I admit, I would have my doubts if I had not experienced the same thing.

Years before 2016, it seemed as if the decision to vote for a president was solely up to me. I said, "God doesn't pick presidents, He leaves that in voter's hands." "Whatever we decide He works with knowing who we will pick in advance because He is God." However, it appeared God had taken a greater interest in the last few elections by directing many people on whom to choose.

I had never heard before, so many people tell me it had been revealed to them who to choose for president. This must have been one of the most important elections in the history of our country. Regardless of why other people ultimately voted for Trump, this was one of the reasons certain people backed him. They believed Donald J. Trump was called, chosen, and appointed by God to be the United States President.

REASON #18

HE IS FULFILLING PROPHECY

Certain people are completely amazed at all of the prophecies about Trump. They say, they have never heard of anything like this before. Whether on the local, national, or international level, men and women around the world who have a reputation for being accurate prophets, were stating that God had chosen this man to be president, some mentioned for two terms. There is one in particular that comes to mind, that even prophesied about the impeachment attempt and failure many years before it ever happened; in addition to many other events that are now occuring. I researched and couldn't find one known prophet with an opposing word mentioning that the competitor had been chosen by God instead.

Many faith-based voters believe the prophets have spoken accurately. It appears that the prophets may have been mistaken about this re-election. However, there are those who believe that when the matter has been thoroughly investigated, it will reveal the truth and prove these prophets have been divinely inspired.

REASON #19

HE SUPPORTS ISRAEL

There are many Trump supporters who believe whoever blesses and stands with Israel will be blessed. Many are excited to have the friendliest, most supportive president ever for Israel helping them while they pray for peace in Jerusalem. Trump has favored Israel on just about every diplomatic situation. He has taken steps to place restrictions on Israel's enemies. Most deals concerning Israel are supported.

Trump has changed previous U.S. policies on important security, diplomatic, and political issues to Israel's favor. These include the status of Jerusalem and the Golan Heights, treatment of Israel at the United Nations (UN), the Iran Nuclear deal, and the Palestinian-Israeli conflict.

On Dec 6, 2017, Trump formally recognized Jerusalem, the Holy city, as the capital of Israel and moved the U.S. embassy there. This was after 70 years of being in Tel Aviv. Other past presidents made promises to do this, but none followed through. While others perceived peace in the Middle East to be a potential threat, a bold Trump made it clear to the world where the U.S. stood with their support for Israel. In December 1949, Israel declared Jerusalem as its capital, but up until now hardly anybody recognized it.

On March 25, 2019, Trump signed a proclamation making the United States the first country to recognize Golan Heights as part of the State of Israel. The United Nations previously stated that Israel's settlement there was a violation of international law and was illegitimate.

Trump withdrew the U.S. from UNESCO (United Nations Educational Scientific and Cultural Organization). He also decided to withdraw from the UNHRC (United Nations Human Rights Council) in June 2018. Trump also ended funding after decades to the UN Relief and Works Agency (UNRWA). All of this was due to what he believed to be an anti-Israel bias. The records show Israel has been singled out discriminatorily at the UN. In the last 7 years, the UNHRC has faulted Israel in 80% of its cases. Trump also backed Israel against the (ICC) International Criminal Court, in their attempt to investigate Israel for war crimes. Trump has been harsh against the ICC investigative plans against Israel and the U.S. He threatened to impose sanctions on anyone involved.

Trump sided with Israel and the Arab states against Iran. In May 2018, He withdrew the U.S. from the Iran Nuclear deal and imposed harsh sanctions on them. Trump honors the ten-year MOU (Memorandum of Understanding) signed on record for Israel which continues to provide the military assistance the USA has always provided to Israel. Israel also provides military intelligence and other services to the US in exchange.

Lastly, Donald Trump is the first ever sitting American president to visit Jerusalem (Holy Sepulchre and Western Wall).

REASON #20

HE DOES NOT FOLLOW THE GLOBAL AGENDA

Many Americans have been concerned with a New World Order, global reset, socialism, communism, and America's sovereignty being lost. They believe the president shares these concerns. Mr. Trump has made a name for himself around the world for his refusal to cooperate with, go along with, and bow down to global world organizations. He made it clear when addressing the United Nations that America under his watch will never give up their sovereignty. America will never be subject to international councils and will always fight for its freedom. It will not yield to socialist or communist control and will always choose patriotism over globalism.

The Trump administration formally began the United States withdrawal from the Paris Climate Agreement. It is made up of 196 countries and supposed to regulate the rise of the global temperature. He terminated our relationship with the World Health Organization which he believed to be corrupt and participatory in causing problems related to the Covid virus. He permanently withdrew from and cut the funding of several United Nation agencies. His Multilateral pacts blocked the appointment of judges to the World Trade Organization, leaving it crippled. He threatened to quit the pacts due to resolution disputes with member countries, unfair rulings to U.S.A, and concerns for U.S. sovereignty. Here are other global decisions made thus far by the Trump administration:

- ✓ He axed the Trans-Pacific Partnership trade agreement that involved Japan, Canada, and Australia saying it was a bad deal for America. We are no longer paying 40% of the global GDP.
- ✓ He withdrew the US from UNESCO, the UN's educational scientific and cultural organization, whose goal is to protect the culture and tradition of our world's heritage.
- ✓ He left the Global Compact for Migration which manages safe orderly and regular migration around the globe.
- ✓ He removed the US from the UNHRC, a human rights organization that supposedly protects and promotes human rights.
- ✓ Trump ended decades of funding to the UN Relief and Works Agency due to what he believed to be anti- Israel bias. The majority of funds appeared to aid Palestinian refugees above all refugees across the world.
- ✓ Trump withdrew from several US-Russia arms control treaties, like the Intermediate Range Nuclear Forces open skies treaty. He preferred a mutual arms cooperation between the powers.
- ✓ He weakened and undermined the credibility of NATO, North Atlantic Treaty Organization by publicly denying our adherence to its charter.

During the covid-19 emergence, he did not favor more lockdowns. He did not allow fear to cause him to kill the economy for millions of people and because percentages showed over a 99% recovery. He even contracted covid-19 and quickly overcame it. He has weighed this pandemic and the affect it has had on people and their life. He supports placing people's safety and risks into their own hands. He has the best interest of what the general public wants, not what a few experts and media are saying.

Despite censorship by government experts against Front Line Doctors who suggested and prescribed treatments and alternatives that have been proved to work in early treatment, President Trump defended the doctors who stood on the Supreme Court steps and their promotion of the hydrocloroquine treatment. He was willing to battle against the CDC (Center for Disease Control and Prevention) and Dr. Fauci with some of their conclusions and recommendations.

If we look at how he has spoken up for people's rights during the Covid crisis, this is another telltale sign. He is promoting the opposite of what the establishment and so called experts want to do: lockdown, mandatory masking of all, social distancing, and closing businesses and schools. This leads many concerned citizens to also believe he will not support mandatory vaccinations. His record of support for individual freedoms, moral conscious, and religious liberty causes is the basis for supporter's faith in him.

REASON #21

HE IS FIGHTING THE MEDIA FOR TRUTH

The media attack against the president is only one of many proofs that Mr. Trump may be doing something right, his supporters say. Trump's informed backers know that lying is part of the media's strategy. Donald Trump was not being funny when he called them "Fake News." He was being truthful. His supporters know unfortunately, too many people believe everything they hear from mainstream media. They are bothered by the hypocrisy and slant of mainstream news stations. Trump followers say journalists are experts at painting narratives they want people to believe. They pull on the emotional strings of their audience. Opinionated newscasters steer Americans on what to believe, what is bad and good for us, and what is divisive and unifying. Their goal is for us to think, believe, and act according to the way they want. Fake news is not interested in telling facts as much as it is interested in influencing people's decisions.

"He will never be president." "The world will be horrible if that happened." "I would move out the country if Trump became President." These statements were given by people on the news before he won the first election. Trumps supporters believe America is in a much better position years later (except for Covid-19). Trump's supporters say eventhough the news media lied about the election polls favoring one side, they still lost the vote. President Trump's enemies have not found a way to defeat him, and he takes it all in stride.

People who have taken the time to research and find out the truth, don't believe the mainstream news media. They don't care what is being said, they are convinced of what is really happening. In Trump, they see something the media won't see. They see a protector of freedom and fighter for American people against deception, manipulation, and control.

What keeps Trump and his supporters from being able to fix this onslaught of lies told by our news media? Herein lies part of Trump's biggest battles. He understands, you can never have real freedom without truth. How will he be able to take down such an formidable force? It starts with helping people realize who the real defenders and real enemies are. Trump continually reminds his backers every chance he gets.

RESPONSE TO COMPLAINTS

Character

If people were asked what they want in a president, we would possibly hear words like: **genuine**, **patriotic**, **strong**, calm, transparent, friendly, humble, accountable, honest, positive, knowledgeable, and **confident**. If people in this nation were asked to use one word to describe Mr. Trump, we could possibly hear from those against him the words tough, hard-nosed, sarcastic, degrading, prideful, heated, intense, arrogant, cocky, and racist.

When we consider which traits are extremely important and needed to lead our nation at this time, many might say visionary, influential, resilient, communicative, courageous, focused, passionate, inspirational, and decision maker. These can all be seen in President Trump. We have also highlighted those characteristics previously mentioned that some think would fit Mr. Trump.

Who sets the standard of morality for a president? Who would meet the moral character to lead a nation according to that standard? Positively, to be president there should be certain requirements, but what moral standards are good enough? Every public servant must set this for themselves. Besides that, every voter must then decide whether that public servant passes moral standards to represent them. There are individual voters telling others by their standard, Trump does not meet the requirement. Each person believes his or her standard should be everyone else's. Ordinarily, people of like minds group together, then like a pack of wolves, they attack the target and anyone who tries to defend them.

We should see Trump like every human leader including ourselves, IMPERFECT. We are all framed by this outside world, molded by our experiences, and influenced by our personal world. Trump may be seen at times as what must have been a very rambunctious boy in what is now a grown-up man's body. As with all other men, there will be signs of great maturity in areas with hints of immaturity in others. In all people, there will be some transparency, struggles with temptations, a tendency to hide our weaknesses, and a defending quickly of accusations made against us.

How many times has a child failed in some way? How about a spouse? How about a good friend? Do we hate them or throw them away? We do not because we believe in them and are committed to their success. As parents, who normally have unconditional love for their children, especially mothers, we refuse to give up on them. Mothers keep believing even when there appears to be no visible signs of hope.

As human beings, we have a tendency to overlook and excuse the transgressions and behaviors of those we like, while magnifying any perceived moral defects of those we don't like. Man is a known hypocrite in his judging.

When it comes to politics, the goal for many politicians is to win at all cost. One of the ways politicians operate is not to stand on their own strengths, vision, promises, and accomplishments alone, but to expose and exploit any weaknesses or failures of their opponent. They want to make them look bad while making themselves look good. Almost all political candidates follow this format. This is unfortunate.

As the watching public, we seem to follow this same approach. We forget our own failures and limitations while we concentrate on others. We think we are not like them, but much better. We place them outside of ourselves and feel justified in making permanent judgements about them.

For example, when Hilary Clinton said Donald Trump did not meet the standards of morality and integrity to be president, this was coming from someone who had detailed reports from many witnesses about her own character flaws and suspected criminal behavior against Americans and people around the world. Her flaws were witnessed while she held a high office in politics. This is not to mention public gaffes committed by her husband who served as president in prior years.

This was hypocrisy in the worse sense. This is the perfect example of the scripture verse, "You hypocrite, first take the log out of your own eye, and then you will see clearly to take the speck out of your brother's eye." (Matt 7:5 NASB) Why does it seem that our standards always apply to everyone else, but us sometimes? There is no candidate that would pass the integrity character test perfectly; although there may be some that appear to have a more superior character than another.

Enduring scrutiny as a public figure can be rough and demoralizing. Especially, if they are a mover and shaker. They will be criticized for everything they say. A person who puts themself out in the public's eye, can expect to be criticized. People who are sensitive, are people pleasers, and crave public approval do not have the thick skin needed to deal with public scrutiny. A vast majority of people play it safe and would never be able to endure the abuse that accompanies a public servant. They are unable to handle the stress that comes with the job.

Leadership is not for talkers. It is for those who take the credit for their success and being in the doghouse for mistakes. Those who will own failures. It is easy to be a critic. It is easy to be on the outside looking in, saying what needs to be done and how it should be done. People feel they have the answers to the world problems during talks with friends and family on the phone, at the gym, at work, in front of the TV, and on social media. The way a person sees things, they believe is the absolute right way.

Someone once said, "Opinions are like belly buttons, everyone has one." This is true, but everyone does not have the guts to lead. Can most handle the whole world watching their every step? Can most handle being crucified in the court of public opinion, unable to defend oneself at times? Leaders must continue to lead even when there is betrayal; and they are given up on. They must move forward whether someone is with them or not. They must still bear the ultimate responsibility. The fact is: Many are not leaders. Most would abandon their leadership post in the heat of battle, soon as opposition got wind of a past mistake and used it in the media against them.

Should we talk about all our failures, sex capades, unfaithfulness, less than perfect job history, debt history, relationship failures, secret destructive behaviors, lying, and cheating? Can we stop there when there is so much more that could be added. For many, these are not one-time failures, but repeated mistakes. These may also include things we have done nobody knows but God. The only difference between many who have a prison record and many who do not, is usually one got caught and the other did not. The point here, **Is the hatred, negativity, and continual onslaught against President Trump truly justifiable by anyone?**

Let us say, someone is in the hospital and the doctor says they need to have heart surgery to live. He says there are two surgeons available, John and Ted. John is extremely nice, moral, and decent. Everybody in the hospital likes him, but only 50% of his patients recover. On the other hand, Ted is someone many people do not like. He is mean with a bad attitude. They see him as obnoxious, rude, immoral, and divisive. However, he is a great surgeon with a 90% success rate.

Which one would most choose to do the surgery? Probably the one that will give them the best chance to live - Ted. They might say, "What does his attitude have to do with fixing my heart? I need a heart repair, not Mary Poppins right now." What really matters is, who can get the job done when my livelihood is at stake? They would not see themselves as condoning bad behavior by choosing him to use his skills and doing his job in their best interest. Their other option may seem good, but they will more than likely take a chance with the one who will give them the best chances of survival.

Division

One of the criticisms of this president is he divides people, instead of bringing them together. It takes a skilled person to bring two sides from different places, with different views, to work together as a team. His skills for his ability with this are still unknown for many. However, what is known is there will be no compromise with his beliefs.

The word divisive is used by the media and others to describe people who take a stand for things that others might find offensive. The actual meaning of the word has to do with someone whose motive is to cause two sides to stand against each other. This is not what President Trump is doing. It is not what people want when they take a stand. Unfortunately, division happens automatically when someone takes an unpopular stance. People are forced to choose a side they agree with.

If Trump is a divisive person, then Martin Luther King Jr. would have to be considered divisive for taking a stand against racial injustice when much of the country opposed desegregation and equal rights and saw nothing wrong with it. We would never call Dr. King divisive because of the worthiness of his goal, which was justice. Why wouldn't he just go away and stop his civil right's actions? I'll tell you why, he was a peacemaker, not a peacekeeper.

Peacekeepers are more concerned about making someone upset than they are about doing what is right. Peacekeepers try to make both sides happy. Real progress never happens without someone taking a stand. Peacekeeping is usually temporary and external. It's a way of keeping everything calm for the moment without taking a stand to deal decisively with real issues.

On the other hand, peacemakers realize you can't make everybody happy. Peacemaking is about stating harsh realities, doing your part, and putting others in a position to make their own choices; what they want to do about it. Peacemakers let others know where they are going, what they are doing, and whether or not they want to follow.

This is exactly what a man named Jesus did. If one reads about Jesus Christ in the Bible, they would consider Him a devisive person because many people had difficulty accepting His declarations. He said people in their own families would divide because of His message and their choice to follow Him. Jesus is called in scripture "Prince of Peace." People would never call him divisive. Followers of His, knew His purpose was never to divide us, but He knew division is unpreventable in our fallen world when one takes a stand. His attempt was to bring a real unity and remove humanity from a false sense of peace. We divide ourselves based upon our own responses to His truth.

Jesus said, "Blessed are the peacemakers," not peacekeepers (Matthew 5:9). Peacemakers take risks. Peacekeepers do nothing to move things to a forward direction. People want Trump to be a peacekeeper. This is not the type of person Trump is. Many are thankful.

Radicals in America have changed word definitions to give them negative labels to be used against anyone who refuses to agree with certain ways. They have been allowed to redefine the meaning of words to fit personal persuasions and ideas. It has been a gradual and unnoticeable change. Unless we are able to think critically, we end up being easily persuaded by them.

Unity in America

Is America more united without Trump? Did Trump's message bring disunity? Did it show us where we really are? American unity is a bit of a myth. During what time has America not been divided? Our country has had united moments, but was it ever real unity? Wealth and race disparities among other things, define the past and present. We cannot any longer pretend like we are not divided. We also cannot pretend there will be real peace with or without a certain candidate.

Donald Trump may not have succeeded in bringing everybody together but has succeeded in bringing Americans who stand for

America together. We see, before our very eyes, a renewed patriotism for America. A renewed love and passion for the USA. People have gathered in unity under one banner, where the focus is on the love and greatness of being an American.

True divisors are the enemies of American freedom. It is the goal of these individuals to keep the country preoccupied with fighting smaller battles while they take control of America and the rest of the world. America plays a major role in what happens in the rest of the world. They have been a major player in the affairs of many nations and governments. Therefore, since people are watching what happens to this nation, Americans should unite for the right reasons.

Racism

During the 1970's and 1980's, many families watched the popular sitcom shows, *All in the Family* and *The Jeffersons*. Looking back now, I can better understand why those shows were so popular and why people loved the Archie Bunker and George Jefferson characters. These men were famous although they were considered bigots, racists, and prejudice. Why would people take time to sit down and enjoy these characters? It does not make sense. How could you love these characters when you heard what they were saying and watching what they were doing? How come nobody seemed to be offended? If we were all honest, there is a little Archie Bunker in all of us.

In many ways, more than a laugh or the watching of good acting, it was an opportunity to hear men share what many were thinking, but too afraid to say. These men as actors could say it for us and we could laugh it off without dealing with the backlash and scrutiny it would otherwise bring. It was a backdoor way of dealing with racial tension. It was a risk we did not have to take because somebody else took it.

The stories we hear of President Trump being a racists are predominantly based on remarks made by him of other places, people, and gender. He is guilty of not using the best words on occasions and some ill advised behaviors. I'm not sure if we have heard anything that we haven't heard in the public square, nor am I certain that we haven't been guilty of making comments ourselves that appear prejudice. Are we all now racist? Is it proper to label someone permanently as a racist based on these facts?

Everyone has lied. Should we call everyone a liar? Maybe if they lied consistently. Based on the examples given by media and others, most of the world must be racist, including lots of minorities. We must all be liars as well, especially the media themselves.

A better definition given for racism is someone using privilege to keep others from attaining better. Has this been happening with this president? What strikes me as uncharacteristic for an alleged racist, is that Trump has helped Black Americans get out of prison with his *First Step Act* and helped support historically black colleges with his *Future Act*. He was also reported as having more Latino, African American, and Asian votes during his campaign for re-election.

How come Mr. Trump was blamed for increased racial tension in our nation because of who he is? Did Eric Garner, Michael Brown, Tamir Rice, Walter Scott, Alton Sterling, Philando Castile lose their lives by white officers under his watch or the previous administration? Any loss of life is a tragedy and these losses happened before he entered office. Was the previous president blamed for this? It is also amazing how many groups have formed to protest white on black injustices, which news stations love to report. However, we find no groups formed or news reports to assist or solve anything for black on black murders. Almost four thousand gun violent deaths happened under President Obama's reign in the largest city of the state he once represented as Senator. It is still a problem today. What has been done about it? What publicity has Antifa, Black Lives Matter, or any other organization promoted about this?

Many African Americans voted for Trump because they were tired of being on the winning side of an election campaign, but on the losing side of day to day living. They were tired of seeing party leaders make promises, while their cities became worse. Many people are becoming more self-aware and tired of living a measly existence. They want more than a handout. They want a hand up.

People do not want a paycheck in the mail that gives them just enough to survive, they want opportunity that gives them what is needed to thrive. They do not want the government to make decisions that they believe is in the best interest of the people. Just like African Americans, other minorities also voted because they value freedom and opportunities. For someone to advance, at some point they will have to focus more on what they can do for themselves, than on what someone else may be doing against them.

Immigration and Women

Trump's handling of illegal immigration has posed a problem for those who see his determination to control it as overboard. They seem to think it is not a problem to our society at large. Should the U.S. take a more relaxed approach? Should they be at ease in letting illegals come into the country? How can outsiders take the U.S. seriously if they can maneuver around the laws and make Americans feel obligated to take care of them after entering? What other nation allows outsiders to do this?

Each family crossing our borders illegally are willing to take the risk. Their reasons shouldn't be because they know they can get away with it. The main issue is: How to send people back to their country when they come illegally? People complain that families are separated at the border and this is horrible. I agree, but in the U.S. every day children are separated from their parents by law enforcement or social services due to arrests and abuse allegations. There is no uproar made about this, because people understand how law works. Why would it be different in another situation?

People complained about the cages lawbreakers were locked in. Isn't this what lawbreakers in this country experience? These cages, built by the previous administratons, were placed under patrol officers that were following the same routines. Now under Trump's watch, these routines practiced for years, are now inhumane. Why is he blamed? Is this true heart wrenching care by the media, politicians, and their supporters? Or Is this another manipulation tactic to put Trump in a negative light?

Women

More important than the president's past remarks about women are his actions that have placed women in important positions. As examples were given to convince voters of how Trump devalues women, there is evidence of actions showing his high regard for them. This is evident in his administrative selections. To Trumps credit, He appointed four women to cabinet positions.

Elaine Chao, Secretary of Transportation, is the first Asian American cabinet member ever selected. Gina Haskell, is the first female CIA director. Thirty percent of the federal judges he appointed were women. His last few press secretaries have been women. He also had a woman as the secretary of Homeland Security and White House Deputy Chief of Staff. Helen Ferré, a Nicaraguan American, served as the White House Director of Media Affairs. Furthermore, women have led his campaigns. His supporters believe he deserves more credit for showing a healthy respect for empowering women.

White males may make up his majority, but have we considered he has also fired more white men in four years than any other president. He may not always know what he wants, but it sounds like he definitely knows what he doesn't want.

ROLE OF MEDIA

Smith Wigglesworth of Britain was an evangelist in the early 1900's. He became widely known for his radical faith and the incredible miracles wrought in his ministry. Those who knew him firsthand testify that he would not allow anyone to bring a newspaper in his house. His words were something like, "You can't come in here with those lies, lies must stay outside."

In 2006, me and my children landed on the front page of the San Francisco Chronicle. We were highlighted as a minority family that was home-schooling our children, which was a rarity. The interview went great with the news columnist, however the story in the newspaper was not the narrative we gave. Our words were twisted to say things we never said. This was very surprising to me.

After this, we did a reality show on one of the major networks called *Wife Swap*. We had our concerns, but having received certain guarantees, we trusted the producers and signed the contract. I guess I didn't learn my lesson from my first experience with the media. The show was more about cutting and pasting footage that painted the storyline they had already developed instead of the truth. When I realized what was happening, I began to sabotage my part. I was threatened by the producer that if I did not cooperate, I would be made to look as bad as possible to the world. We let them know they could go right on ahead. After that we did a live interview on Good Morning Sacramento. They attempted to steer our words in another direction, but being live on the air, we were able to steer them back to the actual truth.

I have listened to different friend's media stories. Many of them shared stories of the lies and deception they experienced. In fact, one couple had the opportunity to go on the show of a world, famous talk show host (not going to mention her name). They told her about the lies used to get them there and she said, "Welcome to the world of media and show business." During the taping of the reality show, one of our producer's assistants confided that her job required her to lie. She said she had grown up in a family of strong moral convictions and values and she had lost her way. She also said our family brought her great encouragement to get back on track.

I have heard from several military service men how shocked they were, after coming back to the U.S., to read and hear the press of what was happening where they had just served. They said most of what they saw and heard in the news was misinformation. They said it was what they wanted the American people to believe.

I have heard reports of families who said their fellow family members who were reported on the news, showed photos with the stories that had nothing to do with them. Pictures and videos are used from other stories to embellish a story being reported to make it more interesting for the watcher.

Recently, during one news story on a Covid-19 testing site, there was no one there to be tested, so they used some of the workers as customers to make it appear people were there waiting. Cameras are positioned at a rally to make it look like hundreds of thousands came or just a few thousand depending on which one will match the lie they want to tell. After learning of these things and more, it has made it hard for me to watch or take seriously any of the mainstream media's news without my own investigation.

Too many people do not understand that the major news outlets are all under the control of a few who own those stations. They do not understand the role of media in conditioning the minds of people unknowingly. Without realizing it, the public becomes complicit in their own deception and destruction. The public's repeated listening to manipulator's lies will help them accomplish their purpose.

If we were to study every corrupt regime in world history, we would find that those who have committed atrocities on innocent citizens, limit public opinion and control all mass media. Everything being said is dictated and approved to make sure the people only hear what they want them to hear and know what they want them to know. There is no freedom of speech allowed and individual rights are squashed for the benefit of the government's agenda. Unbelievably in America, we are seeing more and more of our freedoms being taken and censorship happening. We must do everything we can to fight for our rights of free speech and to think independently.

The mainstream (fake) news today seems to blame Trump for everything he does. If you listen to them, he cannot do anything right. He is blamed for creating a climate of hate, for pitting races against each other, for lying about the virus, saying the wrongs things, bad public health advice, and being un-exemplary. If he does something right, the response seems to be not quite, not exactly, you did not mention this, you forgot about this, and what about that. There seems to be something wrong with everything Trump says. The scrutiny is relentless. There is hardly anyone looking through a positive lens. Everything Trump says, is a lie, misinterpreted, disagreed with. Any seemingly mistake is jumped on. Why? Is it who he is? Is it because of what he is fighting against? In his own words, "I am fighting for the American people, this is why they are fighting me."

There is always more than one side to a story. The greatest book that is full of wisdom tells us,

> *The one who states his case first seems right, until the other comes and examines him.*
>
> *Proverbs 18:17 (ESV)*

> *Spouting off before listening to the facts is both shameful and foolish.*
>
> *Proverbs 18:13 (NLT)*

One of the main goals of journalist and news stations is to be the first to break a story, even if they don't have all the facts. They understand that whatever people hear first, is usually what they will believe. The verse above teaches us a foolish person runs off sharing what he believes is true, without hearing ALL the facts (both sides). There are many people who meet this description.

Do you believe everything you hear immediately? How reliable are your sources? Do you research to see how creditable it is? Most don't, because we don't make the time. Unfortunately, quick online fact checkers are not beneficial, because the same people putting out misinformation are connected in some way to those sites as well. Like any deception, some truth may be attached to what is heard, which makes it very hard for people to resist.

Many minds have been trained to believe lies through the lying spirit that governs the mainstream media. It is no wonder Mr. Trump has nick-named them the fake news. He recognizes fake news. He has been calling mainstream news fake from the beginning. I personally know first hand how fake it is, however, it has the majority fooled. The deception is so strong that people can't think on their own and are completely taken over by the foolishness of the media.

I watched a video one day where Dr. Wayne Grudem shared about a study of the major networks, which reported there was about 150 negative comments about Trump to every 1 for his competitor during news broadcasts. The narrative and picture presented is anti-Trump. He is the president that everyone loves to hate. Every thing he does is critiqued. Every decision is challenged. He is called a liar, made fun of, criticized, rebuked, compared to the worst. Every good thing is spun to make it look not so good. Everything is said to work against him. The public is reminded daily, by the fake news, how un-likable and crazy he is. There is no neutral reporting. Any negative news is reported immediately based on non-factual stories, negative press, and disrespect.

Through it all, President Donald Trump daily fights. He speaks his mind and continues to move forward. Like the Everready Energizer Bunny, he keeps going and going and going and going.

We can't fix what we don't see and we can't see what is not revealed. I have been blessed to travel to several nations. People have asked me which nation do I believe to be the most corrupt. I understand they are speaking mainly about one's government. They are always astonished when I say, "My country, the USA." I tell them, "The only difference between us and a corrupt government in the third world is we have the money and systems in place to cover it up." I love my country, but I'm sorry to say it is the truth.

It may be a hard pill to swallow, but it's time we accept that most of the news we listen to is biased without the goal of reporting both sides to get to the truth. The goal is not to report truth, but to make the consumer believe that what it is selling is right and good. This is where they put their hard work at. They work hard to perpetuate lies. Like President Trump, American citizens must continue to expose what is really going on, stop supporting these news stations, look for other stations, and demand change.

Behind the Media

Despite the plan of COVID, which I believe is a created virus, people who have faith are optimistic. Its purpose is to control mankind through fear and dangerous forced vaccinations. We know there is an intervention planned by God to disrupt what is trying to take place. I believe we are fighting against what was planned long ago to be implemented at this time with the help of certain American politicians, rich business elitist, and countries like China. It is not only designed to remove Trump by destroying a booming economy, blaming him for a weak response causing lost lives, making him appear careless and irresponsible; but to implement a plan to ensure election victory by proclaiming the necessity of mail in ballots for our safety, all to bring in a hidden alternative scheme of a global reset.

You may say, "You have no proof." No, I just have my spirit man, Bible prophecies, and research information that points to my thesis of what is going on. Only time will tell all and only God knows all. Even if only half of this is unveiled, it is enough to smash all doubts of non-interference and face the fact that Trump has become a force to be reckoned with. Impeachment, slander, media lies, attempts on his life, and even a bout with Covid-19 cannot stop him. The options his enemies used: cheating, blatantly interfering with democracy, committing fraud against the American people, covering it up through controlled media, unjust court systems, and pretending they won fair and square, shows their ultimate fear of Trump and his followers; and the desperation of corrupt party systems and its followers to force their will upon the American people.

If they will go to these great lengths, what will they do for our good if they continue to sit in places of authority throughout this land. In 2016, Clinton supporters liked to die when they saw the election results. This time around they were poised to not let that happen again. Unable to bear losing and explaining their misdiagnosis, they prepared for the unthinkable in a free republic democratic process; doing whatever they believed was necessary. Nobody goes to this length to get rid of somebody unless they pose a serious threat. What threat is worth cheating for? My guess is: American voters who understand the times and who voted for Trump to stop a global world agenda already agreed on by hidden figures.

CHALLENGE TO CHRISTIANS

As a minister and servant of our Lord Jesus Christ, I don't believe in the idea of completely separating your faith from other areas of your life. The truth is real faith impacts the whole life. It affects how you think, how you perceive, and what you believe. Politics and faith are impacted by one another. As a community member of faith, I should not abdicate my responsibility as a citizen regarding decisions that will affect my daily life and that of my offspring. What is the purpose of prayer, ministry, and church if it does not ultimately impact the people in our cities and how we live our lives?

Donald Trump being chosen and appointed by God to lead this nation is not a personal opinion, belief, conviction, or preference based solely on my thoughts and understanding. It was a revelation given to me by Him. Before 2016, I had never received any specific direction by God for a political candidate.

Before the election in 2016, I had decided I would not vote for either major candidate. One morning, a few months before the vote, God spoke clearly to me and I never forgot the words I heard that day: "Do you think I knew who the disciples were before I chose them? Do you think I knew who Judas was before I chose him?" (Judas was a thief and betrayer) "Why did I still choose him?" I said, "I guess you needed him to do his part to help accomplish your plan." The Lord responded, "Exactly, in the same way I have chosen Donald J. Trump so he would accomplish my purpose." God made it clear to me this was His will. It would now be up to me how I responded to this. I decided not to question Him or argue, but just follow and obey. It was afterward that my eyes were opened to see what was happening in our nation and what God wanted to do about it through this man Trump. I was able to see at that moment, the assault against him was more spiritual than anything else.

Moses was selected as a deliverer, Mary chosen to give birth to Jesus, Esther raised as a queen to save her people, Cyrus appointed to pave the way for God's people to rebuild, and even Nebuchadnezzar was used by God to judge Israel as prophesied by Jeremiah. All these people were put in place to accomplish what God wanted.

Why is it so easy for some Christians to believe God can select Judas to be one of his disciples, but he can't choose Trump to be a tool he uses as president of the USA? Sure, God can use anybody, anytime, anywhere, but He chooses who he wants to use. He told His disciples, "You did not choose Me, but I have chosen you." (John 15:16) He is intentional because He knows who you are, how He has made you, and where He needs you. He does nothing by accident. Why did He choose Saul and David as the first two kings of Israel, if anyone would do? He was very specific, even skipping over each of the brothers to single them out. Only David was ready to fight Goliath and only Donald Trump to fight the giants of globalists and fake media and rise victorious.

Goodness

The greatest struggle in this situation is taking our eyes off God and putting them on humanity. We have forgotten that no one is good but God. (Ecclesiastes 7:20, Romans 3:12, Luke 18:19) God didn't choose us as His children because we were good. I have done many things I regret and some that I would be truly embarrassed for people to know and so have you. God still called and chose me as He has many of you. He did this based on His love and what He knew we could become with His never ending faithfulness and kindness.

God did not choose Trump because he is a good person, no more than God chose us because we are good people. God did not choose Trump based on whether he was a Christian or not. God is appalled at how many of us, Bible believing Christians, have made determinations for Him based on our own understanding. We believe we know God's thoughts about Trump and the election without needing to pray and seek God.

What happened to the admonition to "Trust in the Lord with ALL your heart, **LEAN NOT TO YOUR OWN UNDERSTANDING**, in everything you do ask God and He will tell you what to do." (Proverbs 3:5-6) How about "For **my ways are not your ways** and my thoughts are not your thoughts **as high as the heavens are above the earth so are my ways above your ways and my thoughts above your thoughts**." (Isaiah 55:8) He encourages us: "Seek me while I may be found, call upon me while I am near. Let the wicked man **forsake HIS WAYS** and the **unrighteous man HIS THOUGHTS**." (Isaiah 55:6-7) What is sobering is that God is speaking to His chosen people here, not people who don't claim to know Him.

Judgement

Don't judge with unrighteousness! Don't judge in the flesh! Don't judge prematurely! Don't judge without mercy! The way we give it out is the way we will get it back. (Matthew 7:2) We will reap not only from men, but from God. All we must do is look at the story about what the unmerciful servant did to a man who owed him after he had been forgiven of a greater debt. (Matthew 18:21-35)

Jesus tells us in Matthew's gospel in my own words, "Why are you so focused on all the things wrong with your neighbor and have lost sight of the wrongs in your own life. You are not seeing clearly. You are a hypocrite. How can you help someone else with their issues without taking care of yours?" (Matthew 7:3-5) God's goal in any judgment is to offer a way to help, before final permanent judgment comes. Our goal in judging seems to be to accuse without desiring any restoration. We want people to suffer because of how we feel. We don't always have a real interest in their future wellbeing. We really need to examine our hearts regarding our feelings about certain people.

> *Therefore, all things whatsoever ye would that men should do to you, do ye even so to them: for this is the law and the prophets.*
>
> Matthew 7:12 KJV

Forgiveness

When I declared what God spoke to me and others about Trump, I thought about the negative responses received from professing Christians who had trusted me otherwise. I realized God was revealing to me something much deeper than I had ever considered. I sensed this message coming to me from the Lord: "They don't trust **ME** that I spoke it and they don't trust *you* that you heard it. It's a trust issue based on the offense from what has previously happened."

There is a spirit of offense due to what has happened in this country around the injustices done to women, Black Americans, and other minorities. One Christian lady with hurt in her eyes said, "I just don't like what Trump represents and reminds me of in this country." As I heard others in my community and saw the actions in black churches (Pentecostal, Baptist, Methodist, etc.), I realized true forgiveness had never taken place. In the oldest institutions and religious structures of our nation, we held a grudge against white America.

We had consciously decided we would never trust them and reconciliation would never be our goal. Any incident happening that could be used to prove why this was justified was welcomed and greatly received. It was as if we needed to keep resentment as a defense for our black pride.

Believe me, it also breaks my heart when I am reminded of the history of horrendous crimes done in America to my ancestors over the last four hundred years. However, as a born-again disciple of Jesus, I have been given new vision. When I look at it through His eyes, it pales in comparison to what was done to my Savior and

Lord, while being crucified for my salvation. While He was suffering during the worst of His mistreatment, He left us an example of how to respond. He said,

> *"Father, forgive them Lord, for they don't know what they are doing."*
>
> *Luke 23:34*

He commands us to, "Love our enemies, bless those who curse us, do good to those who hate us, and pray for those who mistreat us and persecute us." (Matthew 5:44) "If you really want to be like me," He says "And please the Father God in Heaven, you must love like I do." (Matthew 5:45-48) He says we must be perfect in our love for others, just like He is perfect. Anybody can show love to their very own. He says we are no better than sinners who do the same. True love is having the power to love your enemies; those who have hurt you the most. Jesus used stories about the most despised people in society - the prostitute, tax collectors, and Samaritans - to show who needed the most mercy. They needed Him most and were looked down by others because of their behaviors and cultures.

In these last days, Trump is being used by God to challenge churches to finally deal with the offense of racism and forgive. We can truly forgive and still know our value in Him. As Jesus and the righteous disciple Stephen (Acts 7:60) showed, we do not need an apology to forgive others. The religious churches refusal to repent from un-forgiveness keeps them powerless. The worst part is the harm that will be faced in final judgement. If we do not forgive, God will not forgive us of any of our sins. He is serious about this.

When we forgive others and choose not to use it against them and treat them as if nothing ever happened, we are not letting people off the hook. What we are doing is entrusting God to be the righteous judge. We are trusting that He is fair and will handle judgement as He sees fit. The problem is we don't trust His justice. We want our own. We want to take matters into our own hands. We think it is weakness, foolishness, and pacifism to forgive and let go of the past, but we cannot hold on to what God is willing to forgive and let go.

Authority

Tell me how do professing Bible believing Christians justify public ridicule, judging, rebuke, and bashing of the head governmental authority in the land. Which scriptures are they using to support this behavior? I asked this question on my Facebook post almost three years ago right before I deleted my account permanently. The response was quiet. One person said, "That's why I keep my mouth shut if I don't have anything positive to say." Do we realize we will give account for every word that comes out of our mouth? I wonder what God will think when he runs back the tape on our mouths of criticism for authority figures while we refuse to pray for them.

I don't speak against or criticize any candidates I am not fond of. I keep my mouth shut. We are to ask God to save all those he has ordained to salvation. We are to ask Him to use our leaders, whoever they may be, so His will can be accomplished.

In the spiritual realm, God is enthroned in the highest Heaven with His host of angels. They understand rank and order. The fallen angel, Lucifer, with his demons now represent spirits in the kingdom of darkness and they understand how authority and order works. Many governments and kingdoms of this world get it. In the military, they are taught the same and understand. All organizations in the business world understand how important it is to function. Sad to say in the church, with so many professing a faith which is supposed to represent the perfect kingdom of God on earth; we demonstrate the most failure in following this important spiritual principle.

Rebellion to God and His leadership is rampant. It is a major problem that causes disunity and disobedience while making us powerless and nonexistent in our influence here on earth. More than anything right now, we need genuine repentance from those who claim to be born again believers.

> *If my people who are called by my name, would **humble** themselves and **pray**. **Seek** my face and **turn from their wicked ways**. Then will I hear from heaven. I will forgive their sin and heal the land.*
>
> *2 Chronicles 7:14*

I do not like to hear anyone, especially a believer in Christ, attack a government leader. Gossiping, criticizing, complaining, and speaking against any leader is not permissible for believers. Telling the leader of your nation off in your pulpit, to your congregation, is not what God had in mind. Writing an editorial piece degrading anyone in a position of authority is not Christ like behavior. Stating factual information for the purpose of education and intercession is not wrong, but this is not what is happening most of the time. We must learn how to hate sin, without hating on the sinner.

Since so many have disrespect for authority, we speak as an authority when it is not our duty or right and goes totally against God's word. What a foolish thing! When we see things wrong with authority, we are to pray and let God handle them. Whatever God would have us do, it should be done with submission and respect.

During one news conference, I actually heard Trump tell a journalist, "You don't talk to me like that, I am the President of the United States." I have also heard others refer to Trump as a clown. What kind of people and nation have we become when it becomes alright to disrespect the highest leaders in the land? Regardless of what he says and does, we must respond appropriately. We have disrespected not only the man, but the office.

Disciples, who profess Jesus Christ as their Lord, have followed the example of godless men. They have borrowed their justifications. They say things like, "You have to give respect to get respect." They exalt human reasoning above principles taught in God's word. This is not a Bible verse. This is a famous quote used to express a thought. Many of these well-known quotes are not God's truths.

We have followed the world system, the secular media, and ultimately Satan in our behaviors without even realizing it, and sometimes without even caring. It's like we have refused to seek after God and ask Him to reveal to us what He wants (His perfect will). Instead we assume with our own intellect that we alone can figure out His ways.

There were times I saw both my parents make bad mistakes, like I have as a parent. I still gave them all the respect in the world because of the position of authority they have in my life. I honor them. Because I loved them, I would always pray for mercy. This is what God's love does; it chooses mercy over judgment. We do not get to select our parents. We can say, I hate they did this or do that, but they are still our parents.

Most people do not disown their parents for their shortcomings, like a mother who never gives up on the child God has given them. If God says so, I should not give up on who he has selected. They are ultimately God's responsibility. He will deal with them as He sees fit. This is what we have yet to understand; we are to leave our authority figures to a higher authority. We are not in position to correct or make a final judgment on those above us. David, the man after God's own heart, understood this when dealing with King Saul. Saul had left God, so God had left him. He was now under the control of an evil spirit. David had the chance to kill him, but left him in God's hand.

What are we supposed to do with flawed people? What are we supposed to do with flawed leadership? I may hate when the president does something I feel is not so good, but he is still the one God selected. God obviously knows something I do not, so I must trust God with him. I must pray and act with honor according to God's righteousness. (Romans 13:1, 1 Timothy 2:2, 1 Peter 2:17) **God never waited for people to become perfect before he placed them in leadership positions and used them.**

I have never seen such hatred for a man and justification for unrighteous indignation. It is as if a spirit is driving this. I'm not surprised, because I believe the spirit of evil in this world already knew President Trump was a threat to what darkness had planned. Human flesh only sees the natural man and his faults. The spiritual man sees beyond faults and focuses on the needs of all concerned. Could it be that God has decided this is exactly who He needed to use at this moment? I believe so, but many people won't be able to see it.

God's wisdom is so far ahead of Man's wisdom. In scripture, God's own people missed the day of His visitation. They missed God in human flesh, right in their midst. Their hearts were captured by other things. Their minds were looking at the wrong thing. I asked God myself, "How come You couldn't just send a guy that was popular with a likable personality?" I believe it would be too easy then. It would not require faith on the part of the believers. I think He wanted to send someone that it would cause people to have to put total trust in Him to recognize.

If God gave us somebody who appeared perfect; no problem, but God gives us Trump. Now our faith, not sight, must work in order to believe and receive the promise. Perhaps it was a test for all of us. So many followed the false prophets of network news and religious spirits, and did the same thing the crowds that followed the pharisees did. They said, "Crucify Him! Crucify Him! We don't want him as our leader; give us the other guy, Barabbas the murderer, instead." Think about it: They really didn't want Barabbas, the only other option the Roman government gave them. They took him because they hated Jesus. They only took him because he was not the other guy which happened to be God's choice for our salvation.

Prophecy

Prophecy is God's spoken words. It was how the Bible came into being. 2 Peter 1:20-21(NLT) says,

> *Above all, you must realize that no prophecy in Scripture ever came from the prophet's own understanding or human initiative. No, those prophets were moved by the Holy Spirit, and they spoke from God.*

Contrary to what many churches believe today, spirit filled Christians believe God has not stopped speaking. The gift of prophecy and office of the prophet never ceased as evidenced by the Holy Bible (Acts 11:28, 1 Timothy 1:18). God speaks today to connect us with what is happening right now with his total plan and purpose. He wants man to know what His will is so we can pray it. This includes both what He has written and is speaking. One is known and the other is revealed. One is general and the other is more specific. One is always and the other is for right this minute. One is for a group and the other may be for an individual.

God reveals to us what He wants to do on the earth through his prophets.

> *Indeed, the Sovereign Lord never does anything until he reveals his plans to his servants the prophets.*
>
> *Amos 3:7*

Our job is to agree with him and stand. He said, "Believe His prophets, and you shall prosper." (2 Chronicles 20:20) The prophet plays an important role through the church - God's agent for change in the earth. Like I said, many churches do not believe this even though scripture is clear on the role of prophets in the New Testament church (Ephesians 2:20,3:5,4:11 and 1 Corinthians 12:28,14:32).

Our world is filled with religious clergy and others who disagree based on their own evaluation and interpretation, but none of these religious workers will claim they have received a direct word from the Lord about God's will concerning Donald J. Trump. When it comes to those who spend hours in prayer, days in fasting, studying Gods word, and continually in his presence listening for his voice and seeking his direction, it shouldn't be a surprise that they can hear God clearly.

A man's opinion will never be able to overtake another's personal experience. Prophets not only prophesied Trump's win in 2016, but several also said it would be for two terms. Despite the world being told he did not prevail in 2020, I still believe God has the last word. The crime, thievery, lies, and deception that was involved in this recent election will be exposed. The light will reveal everything that is in the dark. Justice will prevail showing God is always accurate. The Bible tells us, "Let God be true and every man a liar." (Romans 3:4). I can see a few people not hearing God's voice correctly and getting something wrong, but not so many of the seasoned prophets of our day.

Politics and Church

There is a group of Christians who believe in the idea that we should not get involved in any political matters, but let things play out while we just focus on sharing the gospel message. They insist that bringing these matters into the house of faith causes division. On the surface, it sounds good and spiritual, but unfortunately it is not Biblical. I agree God is not concerned with politics, but He does get involved with government. We are told in scripture that government was instituted by Him and we should pray for government leaders. We are to be a witness for Him to governments. God is everywhere and wants His influence everywhere from the government to the media to the business world.

In the Old Testament, the leaders of governments called for the prophets to find out God's will. Jonah was sent to a city whose leaders repented at his message. Queen Esther did not sit idly by when her people were in danger but asked them to fast and pray before making her appearance to the King. Daniel and Joseph served in Babylon and Egypt in high positions of government as great witnesses for God. God gave them dreams and interpretations that helped those nations avert disasters, saving the lives of many. Jeremiah preached that Israel should repent, but also that King Nebuchadnezzar would be used by God in judgement against them and their land if they did not. It happened just like he said.

In the New Testament, God sent the disciples as witnesses to the government leaders, especially Paul various times. There are many stories throughout scripture that tie both together. When God gives His church directives through His leaders (Apostles and Prophets), they must be bold, courageous, and follow regardless of who does not understand. I would never publicly support a candidate from a pulpit unless I received a word from God to do so. There is a big difference between getting people to follow my opinion versus what God is saying. If God said it, He is responsible for proving it. Some people are thinking, "How do you know if it is really God?" The leader might be using God when it's really his personal preference. We must decide then whether we trust that leader, along with our own prayers to God.

There are those who say people are looking to Trump as the savior of America and perhaps the world. They suggest those who support and protest for him might be resisting the will of God without realizing it. Their views are based on the belief no one can be sure of what is really supposed to happen.

This "what if God is doing this" or "what if God really wants this," is based on doubt. Those who know what God has said and received by God's spirit what they should do about it, are able to move forward without doubt, guessing, and questions.

> *If any of you lacks wisdom, let him ask God…but let him ask in faith, with no doubting, for the one who doubts is like a wave of the sea that is driven and tossed by the wind. For that person must not suppose that he will receive anything from the Lord, he is a double minded man, unstable in all his ways.*
>
> *James 1:5-8 (ESV)*

The ones not sure seem to be at odds with those who say they are sure and believe with all their heart what God is saying and doing. If those opposed are staying focused on the great commission as they suggest others do, should it matter so much to them how others are proceeding in this matter?

Some people have suggested that many have made Trump an idol. They have placed too much faith in a man. I am sure this could be the case for some. Those who understand this is a spiritual battle, know if God does not fight for him, it will not matter. They have not placed him upon a pedestal. They know God has used many before him. He is only a vessel.

ELECTION FOR FREEDOM

With Trump, many of us know what we are getting. With his opposition and rivals, we know what we are getting as well. We are fully convinced it is much worse. Under his presidency, we know we can still live and recover. With his opponents, we believe our nation would be doomed, although we would escape spiritually because of our faith in God. We know we would have to endure the unnecessary tragedy of seeing those around us whom we love, suffer permanent harm. With Trump, we would have a future for our grandchildren, amidst any division. With his opponents, our children's future would be under the control of mandated government rules. After evaluating everything, I determined that Trump represents freedom and liberty for all Americans.

If the convictions some hold about this president being a racist, a divider, and so on was true, which I do not believe, many could still live with it. Yes, many would rather not live with such, but we have somehow still lived our life well already dealing with this. I have lived without health coverage, I have lived with racism and division, I have served under leaders with defected character traits whether in my work, on my jobs, at churches, and in other positions. However, what I cannot do is live under leadership that will remove basic freedoms that allow me to be me. This is what is at stake and the reason so many in America have gotten behind Donald J. Trump, the people's freedom fighter. Many don't see the threat of freedom being taken, but others of us see it all around. We the people will do anything to be free.

It was not surprising to watch those who were not Republicans or Trump fans walk away from their regular party of choice in a movement unprecedented called "Walkaway." It was reported that in two years, more than half a million people had joined the movement. People are awake to the fact that they may not agree with every issue and policy of Trump, but they cannot be on the side of extreme behavior, labeling, and intolerance. These were the very things they had accused Trump and his followers of. These Walkaways realized that free thinking and living is not allowed on the other side and they said, "We want better than this."

How important is freedom? It is so important that many Cubans, Latinos, and others from socialist nations, who now live in America, have ignored all the news stories and arguments that have made Trump appear to be the ultimate racist and against minority immigrants. They voted for him anyway. They want to be able to make their own decisions about their lives and live life in their best interest, without feeling they must conform for the betterment of the world. Global unity is under the guise of "what's best for us" when in reality it's a global agenda under "what is best for a few people" at the top.

America and humans around the world have made it clear that at the end of the day, whether black, white, red, or blue; conservative or independent or whatever else, people want to be free.

> *My definition of a free society is a society where it is safe to be unpopular.*
>
> *Adlai Stevenson*

Is it safe to be red and Trump? Is it safe to be able to share your thoughts without being censored because it goes against the narrative of a group of government cronies? Do we still live in a country where we are free from being afraid to speak our truth? Freedom is being able to live as you want, long as it does not take away the rights of another. Life without liberty is like a body without a spirit. Patrick Henry said it best, "Give me liberty or give me death." Many in this country know what freedom looks and feels like firsthand and it is important to them.

FINAL SUMMARY

Donald J Trump is unapologetically a man of strong words and strong opinions. He does not say what is popular, he says what is on his mind. The only difference between him and many others is they think it and He say's it. This is great sometimes but other times, even if you are a follower, it makes you cringe because you know how it may affect people. He has a way with words. At times it can be advantageous for him. However, many of us know that your greatest strengths can also be your greatest weakness. Have you ever thought how the things that made you love a person, were at times, what irritated you most about them?

The charismatic, magnetic personality that is unpredictable, comedic, bold, and audacious represent strengths that pull you in, while at other times it can drive you crazy. You take the good with the bad. My former pastor used to say, "You must learn to eat the meat and throw away the bones. If you throw it all away just because of the bones, you will miss some good eating."

Over these last four years as president, Donald Trump has matured in his position. I did not agree with everything done or said. I condemn behavior that does not exemplify commonly respected moral and ethical standards. As leaders we know we must be even more careful in what we do or say. Having said that, like many others, I love Donald Trump. I pray for him and support his efforts on practically all the major issues. I approve of most of his policies if not all of his ways. I can't say I can vouch for every action and detail, but my overall evaluation leads me to believe he has the

American people's best interest at heart. He is the great tool needed to accomplish God's purpose in America right now. This will in turn impact the rest of the world.

I did not have this current outlook before God got my attention. I did not feel this way before that. Once I realized it was God's will and I accepted it, I was then able to see the benefits Trump offered. The perception is not mine alone, many share this view.

No doubt there are people who may have voted for him because they believe he represents their personal interests and may have voted for him because he is against the important things they are against. Overall, majority of supporters, which includes a growing amount of minorities and the faith-based world, believes he is the one option in our government given to maintain our personal freedoms right now.

Citizens of America are taking a stand against the world's deep state by voting for Donald Trump. They are standing against communism, socialism, and marxist idealogies. They are opposing global resets, mandatory vaccinations, big government, big pharma, big tech, and a takeover and control of our food industry and natural resources. In order for the enemies of the world to complete their evil agenda, they must have the cooperation of the President of the United States of America, control of justice courts, and enough influence in the government house seats. It's not necessarily Republican versus Democratic, many in both parties have secretly become apart of a greater dark establishment. It is now the American way versus a New World Order. Everything is different in this New World and not for the better as they would like us to believe.

People voted not only for Donald Trump to win for their personal interests, but because they want him to win for America and the world. Many Americans want true freedom to ring in every place. They voted for freedom; freedom of speech, freedom of religious liberty; freedom for unborn babies to live, freedom for economic opportunities to increase, and freedom for educational choices so their children can succeed. In the Declaration of Independence it says:

> "We hold these truths to be self evident, that **all** men are created equal, that they are endowed by their **Creator** with certain unalienable rights, that among these are Life, Liberty, and the pursuit of Happiness."

Many Americans refused to be so stuck on Trump the man that they couldn't see Trump the servant. His supporters don't support Donald Trump for the things he does wrong, but for the things he does right. People don't support him for his past mistakes, but for fighting for every American's freedom, which allows them to do something about the wrong they do see.

May God Bless America.

BIBLIOGRAPHY

30 Jul 2019 Military.com | By Robert Wilkie. "Veterans Win with Trump Administration's MISSION Act Reforms." *Military.com*, 30 July 2019, www.military.com/daily-news/2019/07/30/veterans-win-trump-administrations-mission-act-reforms.html.

"DHS Launches New Center for Countering Human Trafficking." *Department of Homeland Security*, 20 Oct. 2020, www.dhs.gov/news/2020/10/20/dhs-launches-new-center-countering-human-trafficking.

Dwyer, Colin. "U.S. Announces Its Withdrawal From U.N. Human Rights Council." *NPR*, NPR, 19 June 2018, www.npr.org/2018/06/19/621435225/u-s-announces-its-withdrawal-from-u-n-s-human-rights-council.

Gramer, Robbie. "Trump's Foreign-Policy Adventures Haven't All Flopped." *Foreign Policy*, 14 Oct. 2020, foreignpolicy.com/2020/10/14/trump-foreign-policy-wins-losses-over-four-years-china-middle-east-coronavirus-pandemic/.

"Inside Higher Ed's News." *Inside Higher Ed*, www.insidehighered.com/news/2020/01/23/trumps-claim-about-saving-hbcus.

"List of Trump Administration Dismissals and Resignations." *Wikipedia*, Wikimedia Foundation, 21 Dec. 2020, en.wikipedia.org/wiki/List_of_Trump_administration_dismissals_and_resignations.

"On the U.S. Withdrawal from the Paris Agreement - United States Department of State." *U.S. Department of State*, U.S. Department of State, 1 Dec. 2020, www.state.gov/on-the-u-s-withdrawal-from-the-paris-agreement/.

"President Donald J. Trump Is Standing Up for the Sanctity of Life." *The White House*, The United States Government, www.whitehouse.gov/briefings-statements/president-donald-j-trump-standing-sanctity-life/?utm_source=link.

"President Donald J. Trump Is Committed to Building on the Successes of the First Step Act." *The White House*, The United States Government, www.whitehouse.gov/briefings-statements/president-donald-j-trump-committed-building-successes-first-step-act/?utm_source=link.

TRTWorld. *Trump's Top Five Withdrawals from International Agreements*, TRT World, 29 June 2018, www.trtworld.com/americas/trump-s-top-five-withdrawals-from-international-agreements-18543.

Trump Administration: Trump and Israel, www.jewishvirtuallibrary.org/trump-administration-trump-and-israel.

ABOUT THE AUTHOR

Benjamin Marshall is the founder and director of Tell The Truth Ministries and Seeds of Truth Academy. His ministry center and school extend to other nations where he travels regularly. He holds a B.A. degree in Leadership from Bethany University. His other books include:

Time for a New King
Destroying Lies in the Church - Liberia
The Rulers (for children)
Who Created You (for children)

www.ingramcontent.com/pod-product-compliance
Lightning Source LLC
Chambersburg PA
CBHW051954290426
44110CB00015B/2238